"This booklet is particularly helpful in addressing the void in the lives of so many today, especially students and other young adults, whose only point of reference is their own all-too-ambivalent and confusing experience and who have no sense of any binding authority beyond themselves. In a winsome and readable way, Garner shows that ultimate truth and meaning are found only in the light of Scripture as God's Word and that lasting security is realized only in submission to its authority as nothing less than God's own. An excellent resource for guided group study and discussion of these important issues."

> —**Richard B. Gaffin Jr.**, Professor of Biblical and Systematic Theology, Emeritus, Westminster Theological Seminary, Philadelphia

"Dave Garner, in this masterful volume, not only has reaffirmed the Holy Spirit-delivered Word of God through human authors and hundreds of years as inerrant, infallible, and reliable, but has also, with convincing clarity and courageous humility, displayed the Word of God as absolutely sufficient and efficient for evangelizing the lost and equipping followers of Christ. With freshness, our author both challenges and encourages the church in maintaining our stewardship and Holy Spirit-dependent proclamation of the Word of God as we announce the grace of God to the glory of God."

> —**Harry L. Reeder III**, Senior Pastor, Briarwood Presbyterian Church, Birmingham, Alabama

"In this little booklet, rich in thought and vivid in style, Dave Garner deftly leads us through some of the most important questions that a person can ever ask. He points us to the Scripture as the only place where we will ever find lasting and satisfying answers to those questions. He shows us how we can be sure of those answers so that we may live in the joy of that certainty. If you are wrestling with some of life's big questions, or know someone who is, then run—don't walk—to *How Can I Know for Sure?*"

> —**Guy Prentiss Waters**, Professor of New Testament, Reformed ...ary, Jackson, Mississippi

CHRISTIAN ANSWERS TO HARD QUESTIONS

Christian Interpretations of Genesis 1

Christianity and the Role of Philosophy

Creation, Evolution, and Intelligent Design

Did Adam Exist?

How Can I Know for Sure?

How Did Evil Come into the World?

The Morality of God in the Old Testament

Should You Believe in God?

Was Jesus Really Born of a Virgin?

Peter A. Lillback and Steven T. Huff, Series Editors

HOW CAN I
KNOW
FOR SURE?

*To Dan,
As you proclaim Christ by his all-sufficient word,*

DAVID B. GARNER

[signature]

WESTMINSTER SEMINARY PRESS

PHILADELPHIA, PENNSYLVANIA

P&R

P U B L I S H I N G

P.O. BOX 817 • PHILLIPSBURG • NEW JERSEY 08865-0817

Westminster Seminary Press, LLC, a Pennsylvania Limited Liability Company, is a wholly owned subsidiary of Westminster Theological Seminary.

This work is a co-publication between P&R Publishing and Westminster Seminary Press, LLC.

ISBN: 978-1-59638-970-0 (pbk)
ISBN: 978-1-59638-971-7 (ePub)
ISBN: 978-1-59638-972-4 (Mobi)

Printed in the United States of America

Library of Congress Control Number: 2013921768

Life presses us with questions. It forces us to make decisions. Each moment. Every day. All of our lives.

What time should I get up in the morning? Which pair of socks best matches these pants? Yogurt or oatmeal or yogurt *and* oatmeal? Now, that's a tough one. Oh, and should I leave the kitchen window open when I go to work? Though relatively uncomplicated, even these decisions produce palpable pain for some.

Other decisions up the ante. How can I fit exercise into my schedule? Should I drive or fly to Montreal? Android or iPhone? Is this stock a good investment?

Again, difficult as they may be, these questions alight gently compared to matters of more consequence. What school should I attend? Which career should I pursue? Whom should I marry? How will I really know? Will I make the best decision? What if I don't? Will I suffer early-onset Alzheimer's like my father? Will there be a cure in time for *me?* Will this Diet Coke give me cancer?

Now the pressure is on. With their gravity, these decisions at times drop on us like lead weights. They bruise us, brutalize us, and break us, even paralyzing us with fear. One life to live; so many questions and so much *pressure.*

If only it would stop there.

In the deeper recesses of our souls, we face lurking questions, whose answers matter in ways impossible to express. Yet their enormity swells in our souls, and we know that *we* don't have the built-in competencies to deliver a final answer. Certainly not with any *confidence.*

Even some remote questions thump our consciences. Is euthanasia legitimate mercy killing, or does it actually kill the spirit of mercy? What should I do for the starving children in Darfur? Does it matter if I don't really care?

Other questions strike chords of personal vulnerability. Will *I* face God one day? Does he care that I don't care enough about the children in Darfur? Will he care that I had an abortion? Do the Ten Commandments command *me*? What about life after death? Or really, what about *my* life after death?

Ultimate questions with ultimate stakes. Some questions really matter, and we really know it. Their burning prods press and unnerve us. Indecision over their relentless interrogation is itself a decision and merely perpetuates the pain, and despite our attempts to cool them off, these questions ruthlessly sting our hearts.

Is there any release valve for the pressure? Is there a way to know, to own, and to rest in real answers with genuine peace, confidence, and contentment? Can I *know* that I am ready to meet my Maker? Can I really know anything *for sure?*

Before we move on

+ This opening section raises many questions. What areas of life do they address? What are some key differences between them?

+ What makes some of these questions weightier than others? Which kinds of questions exert the most pressure on you personally?

WHAT ABOUT PHILOSOPHY?

While philosophy has tried its hand at the ultimate questions, its inconsistent and dense conclusions would suggest the answer is *no*, I really cannot know for sure. Even a quick survey of philosophical systems and their intramural clashes discloses that philosophy's cartography uncovers no hoped-for treasure. At the end of the day there is the end of the day. And the unknown tomorrow still comes.

Trust in intellectual power (rationalism) leaves us scratching our heads, as our minds suffer insurmountable limitations. We come to the end of ourselves long before most wish to admit. Trust in experience (empiricism) leaves us lost because no one can experience everything, and even if we could, by what measure would we determine which experience answers the ultimate questions? Other philosophical frameworks also come up empty, because they fill our souls with gnawing uncertainty, construing an impassible chasm between reality (things as they are) and perception (things as I perceive them).

This is not to say that philosophy does not get certain things right. But even when philosophers climb to various vistas and glimpse selected dimensions of reality with some degree of clarity, other dimensions they miss altogether. In any case, by what standard is their analysis judged? Who decides what philosophers assess correctly and what they miss?

In the end, even on the highest peaks of human thought we never get beyond *human* thought.[1] Philosophical inquiry left to its own devices births conclusions ranging only between skepticism and despair. When it comes to ultimate answers, philosophy renders its only shared conclusion: *we do not and cannot really know.* Any longed-for hope agonizingly turns to hopelessness.

BEFORE WE MOVE ON

+ What are rationalism and empiricism? How do they both fall short of providing ultimate answers?

+ What is the problem with human philosophy?

+ What is philosophy's ultimate conclusion? Why?

HOW ABOUT RELIGION?

Frankly, religion serves us no better. The sheer number of religions in the world makes determination of a single religion's superiority a fool's errand.[2] Often religious identity is more a symptom of circumstances (where I live, who my parents are) than of penetrating conviction. The irony is, however, that religion has often been held with ferocious, even mindless, tenacity. Nearly every religion has its fanatics.

Tempered by the lessons of comparative religions, the modern era offers a smorgasbord for religious consumers. Now many in the world have opportunity to pick their religion, with motivations for such decisions ranging from personal temperament to sheer pragmatism to moral sympathy. In all cases, they suffer the same limitations as the philosophers—never getting beyond human analysis for obtaining ultimate answers.

The bond of culture and religion further exposes the uncertainty associated with religious decisions: "To one degree or another, religious beliefs have determined the patterns and expectations of all cultures."[3] It is not surprising then to find that cultural and religious relativism dominate the contemporary landscape, with cultural anthropologists often calling us to esteem all religions and cultures equally. Yet the stubborn problem remains. Putting all cultures and all religions on identical footing, in fact, intensifies the agonizing ambiguity of the soul. Both religion and philosophy leave us with our heads banging against a wall.

So what then? Where do we turn? Or, more disturbingly, is there really *anywhere* to turn? Are we cast astray, left alone on the island of our own minds to brawl through life and hope for the best? Are we abandoned to mere fate? Do answers to ultimate questions derive from nothing more than resourcefulness, probability, or luck?

Before we move on

+ In the past, what often shaped religious identity? What cultural realities shape religious identity today?

+ Why does human religion leave us no better off than philosophy does?

THE WORD FROM ABOVE

A brief word is in order concerning the approaches considered thus far. The pervasive weakness in philosophy and religion is that they tender merely human proposals. They operate in a vicious circularity, because the answers all come *from* us. Even the confluence of the most brilliant human minds lacks the resources to deliver definitive answers to the harassing questions of our souls.[4]

If there are answers, they must come from outside and not from within. They must come from above, not from below. They must come *to* us, not *from* us. If there are answers, they must come from an objective and all-knowing authority. In short, they must come from *God*.

Has he spoken? Indeed he has. Before we explore the special way in which he has done so, we must comment on his universal speech. Psalm 19:1 says, "The heavens declare the glory of God, and the sky above proclaims his handiwork." The psalmist, looking at the scope of the universe, notes the perpetual, unrelenting, clear communications from the Creator.[5] God speaks in creation and his governance of the world, and he does not stutter.

In Romans, Paul expands this point, contending for universal accountability to the Creator on the basis of his personal communication with mankind.

For the wrath of God is revealed from heaven against all ungodliness and unrighteousness of men, who by their unrighteousness

9

suppress the truth. For what can be known about God is plain to them, because God has shown it to them. For his invisible attributes, namely, his eternal power and divine nature, have been clearly perceived, ever since the creation of the world, in the things that have been made. So they are without excuse. For although they knew God, they did not honor him as God or give thanks to him, but they became futile in their thinking, and their foolish hearts were darkened. Claiming to be wise, they became fools, and exchanged the glory of the immortal God for images resembling mortal man and birds and animals and creeping things. (Rom. 1:18–23)

Several features surface, but for our purposes we will note only a couple. First, God reveals himself. This revelation in creation—"general revelation," as theologians call it—is plainly revealed (Rom. 1:19) and clearly perceived (Rom. 1:20). God intends all mankind to know him in this way; there is no one anywhere who does not *in this very real sense* know God. God reveals himself personally in creation, and by virtue of his self-disclosure, all men know "all the divine perfections."[6]

Grasping the "god-ness" of God comes to us not by logical deduction; rather this understanding is "given to us, revealed to and in us, implanted in us, by the creative power and providence of almighty God the Creator."[7] To be alive then is to know that God *is* and that I am accountable to him. Consciousness of the one true God is an intrinsic feature of being human. To whatever degree we resist this claim evidences our personal suppression "of the truth" (Rom. 1:18).

A second inescapable truth, one in tragic conflict with the first, bursts forth. In the face of this God who speaks come hordes of *false* religions, in which mankind has pushed back against the creator God, substituting idolatry for true worship and obedience. As such, world history is a religious history, a display of both universal accountability and universal sinfulness. Just as history stages the perpetual speech of God's character, the same history delivers the responding human mutiny—yours, mine, and that of every other human being in history (with One exception, who will be noted shortly).

The types of nagging ultimate questions listed earlier are windows into our God-consciousness. We know that these questions matter *because* we know that we are accountable to God. We know that he alone possesses the answers, making our sinful, self-reliant responses less than flattering. The picture revealed through the windows is increasingly grim: the motivation for false religion is not genuine though ill-informed worship, but rather sufficiently informed but willfully false worship. Human history consists of diverse, yet willful and personal, defiance of the Creator. Our hearts are not a pretty place. And that is a universal problem.

Before we move on

+ Where do the answers to our questions need to come from? How have we already seen this in this booklet?

+ What do we all know, and why? Why are we not always aware of knowing this?

+ What do the numerous religions in the world evidence? How?

THE ANSWER IS BETTER THAN WE COULD EVER HAVE IMAGINED

The answers to our ultimate questions will never come from us because they *cannot* come from us. We are both finite and fallen. We are dependent and depraved. We are small and sinful. We are creature and corrupted. Self-sufficiency wholly fails to address matters of ultimate importance before the creator God to whom we are wholly accountable. In the vicious circle of our stubbornness, we are left devoid of hope before God, barring *his* intervention.

If there is to be an answer, it must come from God exercising mercy. For there to be any hope at all, he must act and speak to us savingly. And though under no obligation, he has done precisely this.

Not only has God created and spoken to us in what he has made, he has acted in grace and explained that grace in words recorded in the Bible. In fact, the words of the Bible come directly into our world of rebellious self-sufficiency, where we have attempted to solve our own problems, to make our own way, and to answer the ultimate questions of our souls *on our own*.

Into the tyranny of this philosophical and religious mutiny comes the word from God, which victoriously, redemptively, and exhaustively answers the torturous plight of our souls. This word, in fact, exposes how bleak our condition really is, delivering both a violent verdict of our sinfulness and the solitary solution to it.

This word comes from outside us. It comes from above. It comes with authority and power. It comes as the written Word of God, the only source of reliable answers, and *graciously* so.

Why is it the *only* source and why should we trust it? In short, because of what it is: *the Word of God*. Let us explore further.

Before we move on

+ Left to ourselves, why will we never be able to get the answers we need?

+ What has God given us, and why is it the solution to our self-sufficiency?

+ What does God's gift to us say about his character?

WHAT IS THE BIBLE?

What is the Bible? This question could be (and has been) answered numerous ways. Speaking about its formal qualities, the Bible (from the Greek, "books") or, as it is also called, the Holy Scriptures (from the Greek, "the holy writings"), consists of sixty-six books written over a period of approximately 1500 years, by the pens of forty different human agents. At the hands of these writers, an assortment of different historical, cultural, linguistic, and educational contexts along with a variety of literary genres combine to produce a deliciously diverse flavor in the biblical texts.

But notably, through this vast historical, literary, and stylistic diversity comes a unified message of how God forgives sinners. The Bible presents no mere philosophical or moral message, but is the gripping account of the plan of redemption promised, accomplished, and applied by God himself. God shows himself to be at work on the stage of history, and with sovereign mastery lays out an intricate plot concerning the birth, life, death, and *resurrection* of history's Protagonist (Jesus Christ). In its multicolored splendor, the Bible speaks with one voice; it uniformly declares redemptive grace centered in Jesus Christ—the only sinless Man who is also the very Son of God, the Savior of sinners.

So when we say that the Bible is the *Word of God*, we mean that its source is God, its message divinely given, and, as God's revelation, its character unlike any other document in the world. This does not mean that the Bible dropped like a parachute from heaven, oblivious to human context and history. On the contrary, it is, as we will see in the next section, an earthy book. But in its earthiness, it is marked by stooping grace: God enters the human context, accomplishes redemption, and speaks in understandable words to explain it.

Yet, though manifestly in human language and for humans, the Bible is nothing less than the very Word of God. While not a novel assertion, it is a sweeping one. The implications of this claim are comprehensive, categorically (re)shaping the way in which we should think about our lives and our world. Or put more properly, as *God's* Word it is to be trusted—completely and confidently. Truly *God's* Word, it demands our undivided attention.

But how can we be so sure? What makes the Bible different from other so-called holy books? What sets it apart from other religious, moral, and philosophical writings?

History attests to those who have believed the Bible unreservedly. To be sure, many have found the biblical redemptive message compelling enough to give their lives for it. Since they understood what Christ's death and resurrection meant to them, the sacrifice of their own lives seemed little to offer. Others, to be sure, have mocked the Bible and its message. As we consider the truthfulness of the Bible, it is surely important to remember that human response does not establish biblical truthfulness. The apologetic[8] of zeal can carry us only so far, as martyrs have died for many causes.

BEFORE WE MOVE ON

+ What are some of the Bible's formal qualities? What is the Bible's overall message?

+ What do we mean when we call the Bible the "Word of God"? What does this mean about how we should receive it?

+ What does the faith of Christian martyrs evidence about the Bible? Why?

IS THE BIBLE UNIQUE?

So the question remains. Is the Bible different from other books? An assortment of arguments could demonstrate the uniqueness of Scripture.

We could survey the Old Testament prophecies and discover their fulfillment in the life, death, and resurrection of

Jesus Christ. The sheer cumulative force of the promises in the Old Testament fulfilled in the New Testament evidences divine revelation and divine orchestration of history for redemption in Christ. The display of divine purpose to forgive sins in a promised Messiah, and the way in which Christ accomplishes that purpose in accordance with Old Testament promise, renders a marvelous apologetic for the uniqueness of the Bible.

We could note the manuscript evidence that cumulatively demonstrates the trustworthiness of the text of the Bible. The quantity and quality of extant manuscripts gives us a clear look at the original writings (called autographs). The New Testament we have now, two thousand years later, is amazingly reliable, as the manuscript evidence displays. Combining the attested assurances of reliable manuscripts with the intricate unity of the biblical message delivers a compelling argument for Scripture's trustworthiness.

We could also consider the *rawness* of the Bible. The historical pattern of writing during the biblical period was often to exaggerate military exploits and kingly greatness. The Bible stands out in stark contrast. Despite any cultural pressures to advance historical propaganda, the Bible does not candy-coat peoples' lives; it does not revise history to portray kings and other leaders as possessing a power and glory exceeding reality.

This is also true of Israel as a nation. Instead of asserting Israel's eminence as the motive for divine selection, Scripture orients us to the God of the nation rather than the nation itself. In fact, through the striking candor at Moses' pen, we discover how the people of Israel are chosen *in spite of* their insignificance and irrelevance. The people of God, according to Scripture, are chosen not because they are great, but because their God is great and he loves them (Deut. 7:6–8).

If that humbling manifestation were not compelling enough, Scripture does not simply distance itself from political propaganda, but speaks in stark realism concerning sin and evil. Even the "good" men in the Bible are bad men. Even the righteous are not righteous enough. The Bible boldly portrays the universal grip of sin in grim ways, showing even the heroes of the Bible as corrupted by evil (e.g., King David with Bathsheba; 2 Sam. 11:1–27).

The redemptive message of Scripture comes with a wholly raw, earthy, and real look at the sinfulness of humanity and provides the single solution to sin—a divinely promised and accomplished remedy in the very Son of God. Truly one of the most compelling features of biblical uniqueness is its realism about sin and its divinely gracious solution for it. Sin is horrid; God himself takes on its horrid consequences as the means of rescuing his people.[9] No other book in history takes sin and salvation so seriously.

Each of these arguments for Scripture's uniqueness has pointed value. Each of them delivers a powerful apologetic for why we should believe the Bible. But despite their strengths, such tactics are not enough. In fact, the cumulative effect of all intellectual, moral, or emotional arguments will fall short of adequate persuasion. This is not because the arguments are uncompelling, but because the human heart cannot receive such persuasion apart from an act of God in our hearts.

This fact has not gone unnoticed, as nearly four hundred years ago, learned men from England and Scotland gathered to summarize the teaching of the Bible. In their assessment of Scripture's power of persuasion, they note,

> We may be moved and induced by the testimony of the Church to an high and reverent esteem of the Holy Scripture. And the heavenliness of the matter, the efficacy of the doctrine, the majesty of the style, the consent of all the parts, the scope of the whole (which is, to give all glory to God), the full discovery it makes of the only way of man's salvation, the many other

incomparable excellencies, and the entire perfection thereof, are arguments whereby it doth abundantly evidence itself to be the Word of God: yet, notwithstanding, *our full persuasion and assurance of the infallible truth and divine authority thereof, is from the inward work of the Holy Spirit bearing witness by and with the Word in our hearts.*[10]

In brief, the amazing features of Scripture are inadequate to persuade us fully that the Bible is the *word of God*. Persuasion is a divine gift of grace, and the Spirit of God works with the Word of God to create assurance too deep for words. Full and final conviction comes to us by the Holy Spirit of God, and to him and his work we now turn.

Before we move on

+ What are some qualities that make the Bible unique among other religious and historical writings? Do these qualities seem convincing to you?

+ What does the author say is one of the most compelling unique features of the Bible? Why is this compelling? Why is this unique?

+ What is the only way we can be fully persuaded that the Bible is the Word of God? What does this say about our hearts? What does this say about God?

THE HOLY SPIRIT AND THE WORD OF GOD

In his final New Testament letter, the apostle Peter warns the first-century church of the dangers of false teaching and exhorts them to remain firmly established in the truth of the gospel. The stakes are high. Peter not only knows the blinding persuasion of false teaching, but is also conscious that lives are shaped and ultimate destinies determined by what is believed. Peter's pressing concern is that the church get its nagging questions answered with the truth.

Read carefully his words in 2 Peter 1:

> Therefore I intend always to remind you of these qualities, though you know them and are established in the truth that you have. I think it right, as long as I am in this body, to stir you up by way of reminder, since I know that the putting off of my body will be soon, as our Lord Jesus Christ made clear to me. And I will make every effort so that after my departure you may be able at any time to recall these things.
>
> For we did not follow cleverly devised myths when we made known to you the power and coming of our Lord Jesus Christ, but we were eyewitnesses of his majesty. For when he received honor and glory from God the Father, and the voice was borne to him by the Majestic Glory, "This is my beloved Son, with whom I am well pleased," we ourselves heard this very voice borne from heaven, for we were with him on the holy mountain. And we have the prophetic word more fully confirmed, to which you will do well to pay attention as to a lamp shining in a dark place, until the day dawns and the morning star rises in your hearts, knowing this first of all, that no prophecy of Scripture comes from someone's own interpretation. For no prophecy was ever produced by the will of man, but men spoke from God as they were carried along by the Holy Spirit. (2 Peter 1:12–21)

After Jesus' resurrection and just before his departure from earth, Peter found himself in a one-on-one encounter with the Master Teacher (John 21:15–19). Having publicly denied his association with the Lord three times on the night of Jesus' betrayal (Luke 22:54–62), Peter now finds himself as the recipient not of a sharp rebuke, but of direct yet compassionate shepherding by the very One he rejected. In this conversation, Jesus calls Peter to love him by caring for his "sheep,"[11] that is, the church—the people of faith in Jesus Christ. The task entrusted to Peter as an apostle is that of shepherd. To love Jesus is to love his sheep.

It is evident in Peter's writings that he never forgot this privileged calling as Jesus' "under-shepherd"; he feeds and leads the sheep and calls other church leaders to do the same (1 Peter 5:1–5). Harkening to the Chief Shepherd's exhortation and model, Peter evidently gave his own life serving the sheep.[12] But not even his death would put an end to his shepherding.

Seeking to perpetuate faithful care for Christ's sheep even as he anticipates his own "departure" (2 Peter 1:12–15), he directs these sheep to pasture where they may graze safely and confidently. Just as he had relied upon the Scriptures in his preaching and teaching as the means of authoritative speech to the people of God (Acts 2:14–36; 3:11–26), in his final apostolic letter, Peter calls the sheep to rely unreservedly upon the Word of God. The particular manner in which he does so is arresting.

Having relayed his own riveting experience at the Mount of Transfiguration, where he witnessed a preresurrection vision of the glorified Christ and heard the voice of God the Father expressing approval of his own Son (Luke 9:28–36), Peter orients his readers to the same mighty voice of God, captured permanently in the "prophetic word" (2 Peter 1:19).[13] In fact, he urges his readers to an unqualified trust in this Word. The voice of God is self-attesting.[14] There is nowhere else to go nor could there be any possible need for verification. When a lion roars, one does not wonder if it was a mouse.

Peter's pastoral heart glows warmly. While his readers will soon no longer enjoy personal apostolic ministry after the close of the apostolic age, he assures them they have a vital source of certain and reliable truth. Prophetic and apostolic word persists in Scripture. To ensure their protection and care, he points them *away* from experiences (even those as heart-pumping as hearing the voice of God when Jesus' face was gloriously transfigured) and *toward* the written revelation of God. Peter points the sheep to the Scriptures.

Why does Peter display such confidence in the Bible? Why does he urge the church toward Scripture in the face of his departure and the always imminent threat of false teaching (2 Peter 2:1–3)? The reason is singular and explicit. Peter commends the church to the Bible because of *what the Bible is*.

To bring his point home, he categorically denies that the Scriptures are a human creation. Contrary to what some of both Peter's day and our own age infer, the words of Scripture do not come from man by either origin or interpretation. The writing of Scripture comes by neither human motive nor human creativity. The Bible is neither of men nor by men.

More specifically, the prophetic words of Scripture are not even an expression of the *impressions* or *interpretations* of the prophets about what they saw. No human author simply watched the amazing acts of God and then wrote what he thought about what he saw. Scripture is no mere human witness to God's mighty acts.

It is much more than that. The "prophetic word" (2 Peter 1:19) has a supreme and divine quality, giving it a character *unlike any other book*. Peter does not concern himself with the precise mechanics of the Holy Spirit's direction of the human author; he does not specify *how* the Spirit interfaced with the human writer. Rather, he describes something much more poignant and critical.

He explains how the words of Scripture come by the Spirit of God, so that the written product is not of human but of divine origin. So while the human writers indeed took pen in hand, the words they wrote are wholly God's words. To demonstrate the Bible's supreme reliability, Peter paints a word picture. Employing the language of a sailing vessel whose sail is filled and is carried along by the wind, Peter describes the prophets as men "carried along" (2 Peter 1:21) by the Holy Spirit.

The men's sails are hoisted, and the Spirit fills them, guiding them to the destination God determined and desired. Human agency is real, but the product of Scripture is wholly divine. The Holy Spirit of God takes the prophets strictly where he wishes to take them, making the very words written the words of God himself.

In short, the prophetic word *is* the Word of God. More precisely, the words of Scripture are the product of the Holy Spirit.[15] And herein lies the critical point. Scripture is to be trusted because of its Author. To speak of the Word of God is to speak of the Spirit's product, and the Spirit of truth (John 14:17; 16:13–15) operates in and with this Word. What makes Scripture powerful, or "living and active" (Heb. 4:12), is that the words are God's very own.

Scripture delivers a final and vital authority for our complete confidence. It is no product of man, no fabrication of human intellect. It is not from us, but comes to us. It is in the truest sense *God's* Word. "The Bible is the living voice of the Holy Spirit today. This is the structure or pattern of working which the Spirit has set for himself in his sovereign freedom."[16]

It is also the source of *our* freedom, for the one who relies wholly upon the Word of God will be secure. Scripture delivers ultimate confidence for ultimate rest. Jesus himself did not equivocate: "Everyone then who hears these words of mine and does them will be like a wise man who built his house on the rock. And the rain fell, and the floods came, and the winds blew and beat on that house, but it did not fall, because it had been founded on the rock" (Matt. 7:24–25).

BEFORE WE MOVE ON

+ As the apostle Peter wrote to early believers, what were some of his concerns? What was the motive for his concerns? What is his solution?

+ Which is more reliable: experience or the "prophetic word"? How does Peter make his point?

+ What role did humans play in creating the Bible? What role did the Holy Spirit play? Why does this give us confidence?

THE HOLY SPIRIT AND THE REDEEMED MIND

You may still protest: How do we avoid the seemingly inevitable conclusion that *we* are still left to decide? Are we not left irreducibly to our own assessments, our own interpretation, and confined by our own limitations? How do we become convinced of the Bible's trustworthiness?

Surely it is one thing to claim that the Bible is the Word of God, but making such a claim does not by fiat create the truthfulness of that claim. A purely assumed certainty of Scripture makes quite uncertain the purported certainty itself. Is not the argument circular, so that the conclusion of the Bible's truthfulness comes from the very presupposition of its truthfulness?

But such a crude, unreasonable, and deflating circularity is hardly at work here. Let us return to a theme introduced earlier.

Since we are corrupt and sinful people, our sinfulness dwells not only in our hearts, lives, and tongues (stubbornness), but also in our minds (blindness).[17] In our rebellion against God we are wholly unwilling, indisposed, and *unable* to accept divine truth. "The natural person does not accept the things of the Spirit of God, for they are folly to him, and he is not able to understand them because they are spiritually discerned" (1 Cor. 2:14).

Romans 1 indicates that as unbelievers we "suppress the truth" (Rom. 1:18) and have "exchanged the truth about God for a lie" (Rom. 1:25). Such suppression and idolatrous substitution of lies for truth turn us into fools, though we claim "to be wise" (Rom. 1:22). In short, our rejection of God's words in general revelation distorts our view of God and of reality. Such warping rebellion marks a point of no return morally and intellectually.

Having already described this pervasive corruption, we noted the wholly undeserved gift of God's Word. He comes to us graciously and discloses to us forgiveness in the Son of God. His Word is a redemptive Word, and by faith in Jesus Christ—the Protagonist of Scripture[18]—our eyes are opened to the real and glorious hope of the gospel. We see Jesus for who he really is. We also have our eyes peeled to the truths and truthfulness of Scripture. Such understanding is entirely a gift. It is not a production of our wills or our minds. It simply cannot be.

In the Second Epistle to the Corinthians, the apostle Paul explains this fact by way of the "impossible" task of gospel ministry. Why is it impossible? Because human hearts are blind, recalcitrant, and humanly irretrievable. Paul and his fellow apostles were fully aware that human words were positively insufficient to bring any sort of spiritual renewal. If it were not for the divine nature of the gospel and the work of the Holy Spirit, Paul and his fellow preachers were pitiable fools![19] What instead compelled them to preach was the divine and personal power of the Word of God to bring about change.

> Therefore, having this ministry by the mercy of God, we do not lose heart. But we have renounced disgraceful, underhanded ways. We refuse to practice cunning or to tamper with God's word, but by the open statement of the truth we would commend ourselves to everyone's conscience in the sight of God. And even if our gospel is veiled, it is veiled to those who are perishing. In their case the god of this world has blinded the minds of the unbelievers, to keep them from seeing the light

of the gospel of the glory of Christ, who is the image of God. For what we proclaim is not ourselves, but Jesus Christ as Lord, with ourselves as your servants for Jesus' sake. For God, who said, "Let light shine out of darkness," has shone in our hearts to give the light of the knowledge of the glory of God in the face of Jesus Christ. (2 Cor. 4:1–6)

Into the darkened circularity of our sinful reasoning shines the Holy Spirit of God, who beams in with redeeming, unfailing, and wholly satisfying truth! God removes the blinders from our eyes and brings us from darkness to light.[20]

So, here is what happens. We hear the Scriptures and the Spirit of God, Scripture's Author, opens our heart and mind. By the instrument of faith, this Spirit gives light to our minds concerning the gospel of Jesus Christ and the words of Scripture. This point bears restatement: the Holy Spirit works in us, bringing about this change. The Spirit who gave the prophets and the apostles the Scriptures is the same Spirit who convinces us of their reliability.[21] By the ministry of the Spirit of God, we now know what we *could not* know. We see what we *could not* see. The Spirit of God shines in our hearts this spiritual understanding.[22]

We turn once again to the New Testament. In his First Epistle to the Corinthians, the apostle Paul speaks directly about this Spirit-wrought change in us that enables us to understand the Word of God:

> But, as it is written, "What no eye has seen, nor ear heard, nor the heart of man imagined, what God has prepared for those who love him"—these things God has revealed to us through the Spirit. For the Spirit searches everything, even the depths of God. For who knows a person's thoughts except the spirit of that person, which is in him? So also no one comprehends the thoughts of God except the Spirit of God. Now we have

24

received not the spirit of the world, but the Spirit who is from God, that we might understand the things freely given us by God. (1 Cor. 2:9–12)

How then are we persuaded? Answering this very question Reformer John Calvin properly directs us away from human rationality, as it is simply inadequate.

> Enlightened by his power we believe that Scripture is from God, not on the basis of our own judgment nor that of others; but, rising above human judgment, we conclude with absolute certainty, as if we saw God's own majesty present in it, that it came to us by the ministry of men from God's very mouth.... It is a conviction which does not call for rational proofs; a knowledge with which indeed the mind rests more securely and steadily than in any rational proofs; an awareness which can only be born of heavenly revelation. I speak only of what every believer experiences, save that my words fall far short of a just account of the matter.[23]

The conviction about Scripture's truthfulness is no mere human phenomenon. It cannot be reduced to probabilities, proofs, or evidences. Certainty cannot come by reasoning, but instead takes root in our hearts by the work of the Holy Spirit himself. Such conviction is not irrational; it is *supra* rational, that is, it exceeds our powers of rationality.[24]

So then, the Spirit who produced the Scripture by the agency of the prophets and the apostles is the very same Spirit who illumines us to receive the Scripture as wholly true. Note well that the Spirit does not change the Scripture; he changes *us* and opens our minds and hearts to Scripture's truth. He enters the closed circle of our rebellion and blindness, in which we rely upon our finite and *sinful* intellect, and delivers us from our self-absorbed darkness into his grace-filled light.

Before we move on

+ What circular reasoning might seem to be at play here? Are we the ones who must ultimately confirm the trustworthiness of Scripture?

+ Can human beings achieve spiritual renewal on their own? Why or why not? When the Scriptures are incomprehensible to us, what must change and how?

+ What is the difference between rationality, irrationality, and *supra* rationality? Which is most reliable?

THE BIBLE IS TRUE AND TRUSTWORTHY: A GIFT AND A MANDATE

We conclude with a reminder of our opening questions. Rejecting the closed circle of human reason, we have exposed an entirely different Source for understanding ultimate questions. The answers to such questions come not from within (by human ingenuity), but from without (by divine intervention). Understanding comes by divine, gracious, and redemptive intrusion. How? *By the Spirit of the Word working with the Word of the Spirit*.

Why is this persuasion so persuasive? Because it is *God's* work with *God's* Word. Scripture possesses unqualified authority and delivers unqualified confidence because of its supreme Author. God the Spirit takes his revealed Word, opens our eyes to it, and mercifully and persuasively seals it on our hearts. Only when we have our minds and hearts opened to the truthfulness of Scripture do we find peace, confidence, and contentment.

Scripture then does not present some parallel alternative, adding to the smorgasbord of human postulates—philosophical, religious, or otherwise. It brings the only answer, the divine one. The decision has already been made. God answers ultimate questions ultimately. He could do no less. His Word is truth and there is no real competition. The Lion has roared and we hear his mighty voice.

As the Word of *God*, the Bible accordingly requires our full allegiance and provides the authoritative source for addressing ultimate questions. This gracious gift serves as a divine mandate. Any resistance to this Word is a culpable resistance, a continuation of the rebellion condemned in Romans 1. To say no to the divine rescue in the divine Word is to act in final obstinacy. It is to remain in the darkness and to complain that we cannot see.

The Bible does not give answers to every single question. It does not tell me whom to marry. It does not convey whether I am to become a painter, a pilot, or a plumber. It does not provide formularies for fantasy football or maps to Montana. It does not disclose the periodic table or the best (or any!) recipe for chicken potpie. The Bible does not speak *about* everything. It does, however, speak *to* everything. Scripture, properly understood by spiritual eye-opening (called "illumination"), gives the authoritative basis by which we must think about all things.[25] It is the one corrective lens for interpreting life accurately, consistently, and faithfully.

By any accounting, Scripture's reliability is simply staggering in both its power and its grace. The Creator mercifully does not leave us to our own devices. We are not left to the inadequacies of human postulations. We are not left in the darkness of our willful, religious rebellion. We are not even left in the realm of probabilities and possibilities. We are not left to wander as lost sheep.

No, God has intervened. The persuasion of his Spirit about the gospel and his Word compels us unto belief, grips us with divine grace, and draws us to a place of blessed rest. The very Word of God, which Peter commends to Jesus' sheep, supplies perfectly safe ground for feasting, nourishment, and protection— for today and tomorrow. Ultimate questions receive ultimate answers. Today and tomorrow are blanketed in divine promise and divine protection. Dwelling in God's grace, we know *for sure*.

A final word of caution is in order. It is by the Word of God and the Spirit of God that we possess the sufficient resources for life: "His divine power has granted to us all things that pertain to life and godliness, through the knowledge of him who called us to his own glory and excellence" (2 Peter 1:3). Such divine intentionality for our provision drips with grace and kindness. For those in Western culture, which idolizes the individual, this point needs to be understood in the shared way Scripture presents it.

The Spirit is not a private guide, but the church's guide. Scripture is a book not for private interpretation, but for churchly interpretation. The Spirit guides the church to think rightly about what *we* read, what *we* think, and what *we* experience. The Spirit of Christ is the Spirit of the church, and the divine gift of understanding is not an individualistic matter. Provisions are for the church, and the Spirit's work is always Christ centered and church applied. "He who has an ear, let him hear what the Spirit says to the churches" (Rev. 3:22).

We can do little better than close with the prayerful words of Ulrich Zwingli, the influential figure of the Swiss Reformation, whose undying love for God's Word shaped his reforming efforts in Zurich and captured his own soul with divine confidence:

> When you find that the Word of God renews you, and begins to be more precious to you than formerly when you heard the doctrines of men . . . when you find that it gives you assurance of the grace of God and eternal salvation . . . when you find that it crushes and destroys you, but magnifies God himself within you . . . when you find that the fear of God begins to give you joy rather than sorrow, it is a sure working of the Word and Spirit of God. May God grant us that Spirit.[26]

In conclusion

+ Where do we find the answers to our questions: within or without? Why is this necessary?

+ What is the relationship between the Holy Spirit and God's Word? What makes this so vital?

+ Earlier in this booklet, the author discussed rationalism and empiricism in philosophy. Are these tools that we use in interpreting the Bible? Why or why not?

+ What did the author mean by calling the Bible *authoritative*? Why is this true?

+ What is the difference between speaking *about* everything and speaking *to* everything? How does this help us as we use the Bible to resolve ultimate questions? How does this help us to resolve less important questions?

+ To whom is the Bible addressed? Who interprets it and how?

+ What do these truths about the Bible teach us about God?

NOTES

1. "The history of philosophy shows the futility of trying to find a solid basis for knowledge apart from the God of Scripture, whether through rationalism, empiricism, subjectivism, idealism, or some other method." John Frame, *Doctrine of the Knowledge of God* (Phillipsburg, NJ: Presbyterian and Reformed Publishing, 1987), 318.

2. We are using the term *religion* here in its broadest sense (all types of humanly constructed forms and patterns of worship), and shortly will distinguish the Christian faith as distinct from the world religions.

3. Richard Pratt, *He Gave Us Stories* (Phillipsburg, NJ: Presbyterian and Reformed Publishing, 1990), 363.

4. "From us" means not only individualistically, but also corporately, as many discern human thinking to operate in a closed (epistemological) circle. That is, knowledge and understanding rely essentially upon human thought on a human plane. In such a construct, there is no consideration of a special Word from God to interpret and explain reality and to deliver answers to the ultimate questions.

5. See Psalm 19:1–6.

6. Charles Hodge, *Commentary on the Epistle to the Romans* (Grand Rapids: Eerdmans, 1994), 37. Scott Oliphint suggests that Hodge follows Calvin here. See Scott K. Oliphint, *Reasons for Faith: Philosophy in the Service of Theology* (Phillipsburg, NJ: P&R Publishing, 2006), 134n27.

7. Oliphint, *Reasons*, 134 (see pp. 131–40). See John Calvin, *Institutes of the Christian Religion*, ed. John T. McNeill, trans. Ford Lewis Battles, 2 vols. (Philadelphia: Westminster, 1960), 1.3.3.

8. An apologetic is a systematic defense of a particular viewpoint.

9. See Galatians 1:3–4.

10. Westminster Confession of Faith 1.5, emphasis added.

11. The image of sheep is a common one for the people of God. Perhaps the most recognizable Old Testament verse, Psalm 23:1, begins, "The Lord is my shepherd."

12. While the New Testament gives no account of Peter's death, extrabiblical literature indicates that he was martyred.

13. By "prophetic word," Peter has in mind the whole of Scripture—especially the Old Testament. But the New Testament is not outside his purview either, because he is conscious of the divine authority given to apostolic writings in parallel to that of the Old Testament prophets (2 Peter 3:2). In fact, he explicitly places Paul's apostolic writings on par with the Holy Spirit–generated writings of the prophets (2 Peter 3:16).

14. By *self-attesting* we mean that its authority cannot be measured by comparison to something outside itself, because as God's voice it possesses final authority.

15. To put it in the apostle Paul's terms, Scripture is *theopneustos* (Greek), which means it is "God-breathed" or God-Spirited (2 Tim. 3:16). Here Paul makes the same point to Timothy about the nature of Scripture that the apostle Peter makes to his readers.

16. Richard B. Gaffin Jr., "The Holy Spirit," *Westminster Theological Journal* 43, no. 1 (Fall 1980): 63.

17. See Romans 3:10–20; 8:1–11; Ephesians 2:1–4.

18. See Luke 24:13–49; John 5:39–47.

19. See 1 Corinthians 2:4; 15:1–19.

20. "It is then from God Himself that we learn the true character of the Scriptures. In the very nature of the case, it must be so. Only God can identify what He Himself has spoken. If man, unaided, could identify God's Word, man would have powers, which are God's alone. And if man

really has these powers, God, whatever else He might be, would not be the One of whom the Bible speaks. We are in reality face to face with the question of theism. Unless we first think rightly of God, we shall be in error upon everything else. Unless we first think rightly of God, we shall indeed be in error when we come to consider His Word. We Christians need not be ashamed to proclaim boldly that our final persuasion of the Divinity of the Bible is from God Himself. God, in His gentle grace, has identified His Word for us; *He has told us that the Bible is from Himself. Those who know Him not may depreciate this doctrine of the internal testimony of the Spirit; those who are His know that God has truly brought them out of darkness into light.*" E. J. Young, *Thy Word Is Truth* (Edinburgh: Banner of Truth, 1963), 35, my emphasis. See John 1:1–6; Ephesians 2:1–10.

21. So writes John Calvin: "I answer, the selfsame Spirit revealed . . . the author of the Scriptures is God. Neither Moses nor the prophets brought to us by chance the things we have received at their hands; they spoke as moved by God, and testified with confidence and courage that God's very mouth had spoken. The same Spirit who made Moses and the prophets certain of their calling, has now testified to our own hearts that he used them as his servants for our instruction." John Calvin, quoted in *Readings in Christian Thought*, ed. Hugh T. Kerr (Nashville, TN: Abingdon Press, 1966), 162–63.

22 While in one important sense this illumination is instantaneous (we did not see before and now by faith we see), our fortification in this divine gift of understanding occurs over time. In fact, the life of a believer in Jesus Christ involves a progressive deepening of understanding in God's Word and confidence in its relevant authority in the face of temptations and pressures within and without. Hebrews 5:12–14 describes the life of a believer as exercise! "For though by this time you ought to be teachers, you need someone to teach you again the basic principles of the oracles of God. You need milk, not solid food, for everyone who lives on milk is unskilled in the word of righteousness, since he is a child. But solid food is for the mature, for those who have their powers of discernment trained by constant practice to distinguish good from evil."

23. John Calvin, *Institutes of the Christian Religion*, 1.7.5.

24. Because sin distorts understanding, divine grace by the Spirit redeems our minds, enabling us to see and to receive God's (biblical) truth with conviction. Illumination is "regeneration on its noetic [the mind] side."

John Murray, "The Attestation of Scripture," in *The Infallible Word*, ed. N. B. Stonehouse and Paul Woolley, 2nd ed. (Philadelphia: Presbyterian and Reformed Publishing, 1967), 51.

25. Biblical authority means neither that everything in the Bible is equally clear (Westminster Confession of Faith 1.7) nor that the Bible speaks about everything. Though Scripture does not address every subject, every subject properly understood must submit to Scripture's self-attesting authority.

26. Ulrich Zwingli, "Of the Clarity and Certainty of God's Word," in *Zwingli and Bullinger*, ed. G. W. Bromiley (Philadelphia: Westminster, 1953), 71; recorded in Jane Dempsey Douglass, "The Lively Work of the Spirit in the Reformation," *Word and World* 23, no. 2 (Spring 2003): 124.